DATE DUE

Be a Better Biker

By Annie Buckley

The Child's World®
www.childsworld.com

Published in the United States of America by The Child's World®
P.O. Box 326 • Chanhassen, MN 55317-0326
800-599-READ • www.childsworld.com

ACKNOWLEDGMENTS

The Child's World®: Mary Berendes, Publishing Director

Produced by Shoreline Publishing Group LLC
President / Editorial Director: James Buckley, Jr.
Designer: Tom Carling, carlingdesign.com
Cover Art: Slimfilms
Copy Editor: Beth Adelman

Photo Credits
Cover—Getty (main), iStock (three others)
Interior—Corbis: 6, 29; Dreamstime.com: 9, 13, 15, 19, 26; Getty
Images: 5, 14, 22, 25, 28; iStock: 8, 10, 11, 16, 17, 18, 21

LIBRARY OF CONGRESS CATALOGING-IN-PUBLICATION DATA

Buckley, Annie.
  Be a better biker / by Annie Buckley.
     p. cm. — (Girls rock!)
  Includes bibliographical references and index.
  ISBN 1-59296-741-8 (lib. bdg. : alk. paper)
  1. Cycling—Juvenile literature. I. Title. II. Series.
  GV1043.5.B83 2006
  796.6—dc22
                          2006001640

CONTENTS

ALL KINDS OF Bikes!

It's hard to imagine a time when there weren't any bicycles. Today you see them almost everywhere! There are different kinds of bicycles for all kinds of riding. Learning some basic things about bicycles can help you choose what type might be right for you and how to stay safe when you ride.

Bicycles as we know them were

invented over a hundred
years ago. The first foot-
pedal bicycles were made in
the 1800s. They didn't look
anything like today's bikes.
In 1871, an Englishman
named James Starley built a
bike with a HUGE front
wheel and a tiny back wheel.

Bikes helped change women's fashion. This woman is wearing bloomers, puffy pants created for women to wear while riding.

In the 1880s and 1890s, a new type of bicycle became popular. These new bikes, called "safety bicycles," looked more like the ones we know today. They had two wheels of the same size, a chain to turn one wheel, and brakes to make them stop. Some also had **gears** (see the box on page 7).

In the early days, girls and women didn't ride bikes much. The long skirts and pointy shoes popular in the 1800s weren't good for riding. Also, many people felt that riding gave women more freedom than they should have. All that changed over time and women began riding often!

Gearing Up

On bikes with gears, lower gears make pedaling easier but don't make the bicycle go very fast. They work well for starting out or going uphill. Higher gears make pedaling harder but make the bicycle go faster. They're best for higher speeds or downhill.

*Bike riding is great **aerobic exercise**—it gets your heart beating faster and helps your heart and lungs grow stronger. Aerobic exercise can help you stay healthy and live longer.*

Today, both girls and boys ride bikes all the time—and so do women and men of all ages. They ride to school or work, to get exercise, and just to have fun.

Here are some of the most common types of bikes:

- The simplest bikes just have a frame, a seat, handlebars, and *coaster*

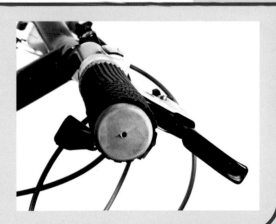

brakes that stop the bike when you push backwards on the pedals. They have only one gear.

- Touring or road bikes are great for riding on streets and roads. They have lots of gears for going up and down hills and going different speeds.

Hands On!

Many bikes have *hand brakes* that you control with two levers on the handlebars. One brake stops the front wheel, and the other stops the back wheel.

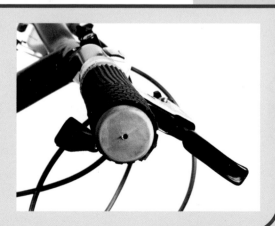

Mountain bikes have very sturdy frames and are made to ride well over bumpy ground.

- Mountain bikes are great for riding off-road and over rougher surfaces. They have tough frames, plenty of gears, and wide, bumpy tires for a good grip.
- Cross bikes (or **hybrid** bikes) are a mix between touring and mountain bikes. They're good for riding on both smooth and rough surfaces.
- **BMX** (bicycle motocross) racing bikes are small,

tough bikes used for racing on dirt tracks.

- BMX freestyle bikes are made for doing jumps, spins, and other tricks. The handlebars and front wheel of these bikes can turn all the way around. Some also have foot pegs to stand on for doing tricks.

BMX bikes are used in freestyle and racing. Most BMX bikes are smaller and lighter than bikes used for street riding.

2

BIKE
Safety

Staying safe is the single most important thing in bike riding. It's also the key to keeping riding fun!

First, you need a good helmet. You need to wear it all the time, even if you're just riding to a neighbor's house. Even the best riders have accidents. If you fall, your helmet can save you from a bump on the head—or even save your life!

Bike helmets come in all sorts of colors and styles, so you can find one that looks good on you. Choose one that you like, but remember, looking good isn't everything!

The chin strap should fit snugly—but comfortably— around your chin. If your helmet is too loose, it won't protect your head.

Make sure the helmet fits you well, so it will be comfortable and stay in place. A bicycle shop is a good place to get help in choosing a helmet that fits.

No matter what style of bike and helmet you choose, make sure they are the right fit for you. Get help from experts to make sure.

Next, make sure that your bike is the right size and is set up just right for you. A bike shop can also help you pick the right-sized bike. The seat and handlebars should be at a comfortable height. You'll probably need to raise the seat and adjust the handlebars as you grow. When your feet are on the pedals, your knees should bend just a little.

Have you ever really looked at your bike, to see how it works? Knowing the basics about your bike can keep you safe.

This type of road bike is something to look for as you become a better rider.

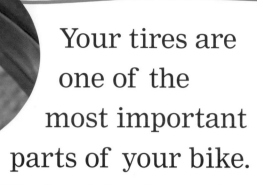

This black tube is called the stem. It is used for putting air into the tire or letting air out.

Your tires are one of the most important parts of your bike. They're filled with air and pumped up to the right **air pressure**. There should be enough air in them to keep them firm even when you ride over bumps. If there isn't enough air, the tires get soft and can cause you to crash. Too much air, though, can wreck your tires.

Every few days (especially if you're going to be riding a lot), check your tires to make sure they're filled correctly. Ask an adult to show you how to use a **tire gauge** and add more air if needed. You can use a big air pump at your neighborhood gas station, or if there isn't one nearby, a bicycle pump that you work by hand.

Bicycle pumps connect to the tire stem by a rubber tube. You pump the handle to put air into the tire until the gauge (the dial with the red arrow) shows the right air pressure.

The chain is important, too. It runs in a loop between the pedals and the back wheel. Can you see how the chain turns the wheel when you turn the pedals? It should be a bit greasy, so it can move smoothly. You don't want the chain to be too loose (it might fall off) or too tight.

If your chain falls off, ask an adult to help you put it back on. The chain goes onto the gears, which are near the pedals and the back wheel.

How do you stop a bike? By using brakes. If your brakes don't seem to be working right, do NOT ride your bike. Tell an adult and make sure the brakes are fixed right away.

Rubber brake pads rub against the wheels to help you stop.

Being able to steer your bike is important, too! If your handlebars are loose, you won't be able to turn your bike, and you might even crash. Have an adult make sure your handlebars turn your front wheel correctly.

Another key to staying safe on your bike is knowing the rules of the road. Many of these rules are the same laws that cars must follow. Here are some basics:

Ask your parents to take you to a bike safety course. Most schools or police departments put them on to help kids become better, safer bikers.

- When you need to cross a street, come to a stop and look both ways—left, right, and then left again. Cross only if there is no traffic.
- On the street, ride on the right side and in the same direction as the traffic. Stay to the right of the cars.
- On the street, use hand signals when you turn. Be sure to obey traffic signals!

Riding in the daytime is safest. If you have to ride in the evening, use **reflectors** and a light that works. Light-colored clothing makes you easier to see, too. No matter when you ride, make sure somebody knows where you're going and when you'll be back.

Look for symbols like this one or for the words "Bike Lane" to find safe places to ride next to streets.

3

WHAT'S next?

Going on a Longer Trip?

You'll need to plan ahead! You'll want to bring water, food, and maybe some tools in case something goes wrong with your bike. Keep the weather in mind, too. Some sunscreen, a jacket, or a rain poncho can come in handy.

Riding around your neighborhood is fun, but as you get to be a better biker, you might be ready for bigger adventures! Maybe some of your friends would like to do more riding, too. Talk to an adult to figure out some fun places to take your bikes. Riding a bike makes exploring new places easy!

OPPOSITE PAGE
Riding a bike can be a great way to take a trip with your family and see new places.

Communities put up "Bike Route" signs to mark places where bikers can ride more safely. These signs usually point out bike paths, quiet streets, or bike lanes along busier streets.

OPPOSITE PAGE

Many national parks have trails you can ride on.

Lots of places have paths and trails made especially for biking. Many of them wind through parks or scenic countryside. Bike trails are great for family or group riding. Trail riding with a group is lots of fun, and it's also safer than going by yourself.

Many people take their bikes with them on vacation, so they can see new sights while they ride! Your parents can get a special bike rack for the family car on which they can load the bikes. Or you might be able to rent bikes on your trip.

Ever wondered how fast you can go on your bike? Try putting a speedometer on your bike! Many speedometers also have an odometer built in. An odometer keeps track of how many miles or kilometers you have gone.

When you go mountain biking, you might run into ground so rough you have to carry your bike!

Road racing is a good way to put lots of miles on your bike! Road racers ride long distances on city streets and country roads to see who is the fastest. If you become a very good rider, look for kids' road races in your area.

Mountain biking is a great way to put on some miles, too. Instead of riding on smooth trails or roads, you can ride on rough dirt trails—or go off-road altogether!

Ready for more excitement? You'll find plenty of it in BMX racing! Riders race to see who's the fastest on dirt courses with lots of hills, jumps, and turns.

In the Olympic road races, men race for 143 to 155 miles (230 to 250 km), and women race for 62 to 87 miles (100 to 140 km).
In one of the most famous road races, the Tour de France, bikers race for about 2,000 miles (3,200 km) over nearly a month!

There's lots of excitement in BMX freestyle, too! Freestyle riders see who can do the best tricks on their BMX bikes. They jump off ramps and over objects, do turns and spins, and pull off other amazing feats. Some places even have special freestyle parks where kids can ride.

No matter where you ride, or how far, or how fast, one of the best things about riding your bike is spending time with good friends!

These biking friends show off their helmets. They also wear other safety gear like wrist guards and elbow pads.

GLOSSARY

aerobic exercise the type of exercise that burns fat, makes your heart beat faster, and gets your lungs working harder

air pressure on bikes and cars, the amount of air in the tires

BMX bicycle motocross, a sport where people ride small bikes on special dirt courses—they race and also do high-flying jumps and tricks

gears on a bike, toothed metal parts that hold the chain and control how fast the pedals turn the back wheel

hybrid a mix of two things

odometer an instrument that keeps track of how many miles or kilometers you go in a car or on a bike

reflectors on bikes, flat pieces that shine when car headlights or other lights hit them, so people can see you when it gets dark

speedometer a small device that tells you how fast you are riding on your bike

tire gauge an instrument that measures how much air is in a tire

FIND OUT MORE

BOOKS

Better BMX Riding and Racing for Boys and Girls
by George Sullivan
(Putnam, New York) 1994
Take a look inside the high-flying, dirt-churning sport of BMX biking, another way some kids get out and ride their bikes.

Bicycle Madness
by Jane Kurtz
(Henry Holt, New York) 2001
This is a tale about the early days of the bicycle and the role it played in the growth of women's rights.

Mountain Biking
by Alicia and Rusty Schoenherr
(The Child's World, Chanhassen, MN) 2005
An up-close look at the popular sport of mountain biking.

Samantha's Blue Bicycle
by Valerie Tripp
(American Girl, Middleton, WI) 2002
This is a story about a girl in 1904 who gets a new bike and how it changes her life.

WEB SITES

Visit our home page for lots of links about bikes and biking:
www.childsworld.com/links

Note to Parents, Teachers, and Librarians: We routinely check our Web links to make sure they're safe, active sites—so encourage your readers to check them out!

INDEX

ANNIE BUCKLEY is a writer, artist, and mentor teacher who lives in Los Angeles, California. She is the author and illustrator of the *The Kids' Yoga Deck* and coauthor of *Once Upon a Time: Creative Writing for Kids*. Annie has taught in grades K–10, and she enjoys working with new teachers.